Charles Flynn Hirsch

Contents

A Harcourt Achieve Imprint

www.Rigby.com
1-800-531-5015

Introduction

Imagine this:

It's early on a Saturday morning and you gaze out your bedroom window as you make your bed. "What a beautiful day! I think I'll just relax and enjoy the morning," you think to yourself.

Suddenly your mother bursts into your room and says, "Hurry and get dressed—we have lots to do before your grandparents get here at noon. We have to get peaches from Georgia, lobster from Maine, sweet corn from Illinois, steaks from Texas, grapefruit from California, and a bunch of tulips from Michigan." And without even taking a breath, she adds, "Then your father needs to get wood from Oregon to make you a new computer desk."

2

You look at your mom, thinking she's been working way too hard—it isn't possible to get to all those places, buy the things she needs, and get back home in just a few hours. And, you're right!

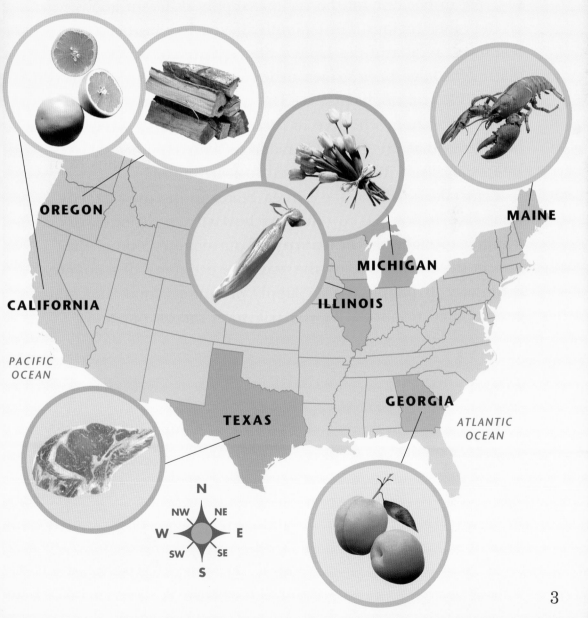

OREGON

CALIFORNIA

PACIFIC OCEAN

ILLINOIS

MICHIGAN

MAINE

TEXAS

GEORGIA

ATLANTIC OCEAN

N
NW   NE
W   E
SW   SE
S

You probably can buy all those things in just a few hours, and you wouldn't have to visit all those different places to do so—you would most likely find them right in your own town or city. It doesn't matter what region, or area, of the country you live in because all the regions supply different goods to all the other regions. For example, if you live in the Southwest region of the United States, you can buy beans that might have been grown in Iowa, which is in the Midwest region. Or you might buy a CD that was **produced** in the Northeast. People who live in these other regions can also buy things that are grown or made in your region. Interesting, isn't it? Do you want to learn more?

Let's take a tour of the United States to discover exactly what each region has to offer and how all the regions work together to make the **economy** of our country one of the best in the world. Oh, by the way, the economy of a country is the way its people use its supply of money, food, and other goods called resources, as you will soon see on our tour.

As we travel across the United States, we'll see rugged mountains covered with beautiful pine forests, rivers and lakes filled with catfish and trout, and rolling farm fields spread out from east to west and north to south. We'll tour a country that was once home to a native people who had their own rich way of life long before Christopher Columbus came to the Americas in 1492. We'll travel through a country of huge cities and tiny seacoast villages, and we'll visit our friends and neighbors who work on farms and ranches, and in factories and office buildings—all of them contributing to our economy.

There's so much to see and so many places to go and people to meet that we'd better get started. Our first stop goes back to the past, where we begin more than 40,000 years ago.

1 In the Beginning

Thousands of years before anyone even heard of the United States, there were people we now call Native Americans living on lands as far east as New York and Florida and as far west as New Mexico and California. These people lived in groups and produced everything that they needed to live comfortably. Some groups grew crops for food, while others hunted animals to eat or gathered foods that grew wild in the forests. These people designed roads and made beautiful jewelry from gold and silver. Many of them became successful farmers, while others were skilled artists.

Native Americans still create colorful baskets like those originally used for gathering and storing food.

As these groups grew in numbers, they began to move from place to place, coming more and more in contact with each other. After a while they began to **trade** with one another for the things they wanted or needed. Perhaps you've traded something like baseball or game cards, or maybe you had two copies of the same CD and traded one with a friend for a CD that you didn't have. Similarly, these Native Americans traded animal hides for corn or clay pots for tools. This is called **bartering.**

Native Americans in the Southwest built multi-story villages called pueblos. Today people in some places live in homes that look like the pueblos of long ago.

One group of Native Americans, known as the Pueblo, lived in what is now the Southwest region of the United States. The Pueblo people lived in villages, also called pueblos, that were built of stone and clay. The villages were usually located in an area where there was rich soil, as well as a river or other water source for watering crops and for daily use.

Early Pueblo groups hunted and gathered for their food but eventually began to raise crops such as corn, squash, and peas. In addition to being farmers, the Pueblo were also skilled weavers, basket makers, and potters, creating colorful clay pots that were used for storing food. The Pueblo traded the items they made, as well as excess crops, with neighboring villages. In fact shells from California have been found where the Pueblo people lived, as well as the remains of pet birds traded with Native Americans from Central America.

Another group of early Americans, the Plains Indians, relied on the buffalo as the basis of their economy. Because the Plains Indians moved about in search of herds to hunt, they lived in tent-like dwellings called tepees, which could easily be moved from place to place.

The buffalo provided everything that these people needed, and never did they waste any part of the animal. They ate the buffalo's meat and dried what was left over to keep for later use. They used the hides for their tepees, as well as for making clothing and blankets. Even the bones were used to make cups, knives, and other tools. If there were any extra hides, the Plains Indians would trade them for vegetables and grain with other Native American groups.

As people began to travel greater distances to trade, they needed something smaller than clay pots or buffalo hides to barter with, so they agreed on items that would have equal value and be easy to carry. For example, beautiful bird feathers, copper bells, and seashells became their wampum, which was an early form of money and just as valuable to early Americans as paper money is to us today.

2 Times Change

During the late 1400s, European sailors searching for a new trade route sailed west and discovered the world of the Native Americans. Eventually some Europeans settled in what was to them a "new world," and they gradually learned from the native people how to produce what they needed to survive and build colonies, which were settlements founded by people who left their native country to live in another land.

Native Americans helped the economy of colonial America from the very beginning. They taught the early settlers how to grow corn and gave them supplies to help them through their first winter.

At first the Native Americans traded with the **colonists** in much the same way they had traded with each other. But the colonists soon realized that many of the things that the Native Americans had to trade were extremely valuable, especially the animal furs. The colonists could ship the furs back to Europe, sell them, and then buy things they needed, like tea, ink, and spices.

The Native Americans did get useful items in return for the furs such as wool blankets, copper pots, needles, knives, and tools, but the colonists definitely made the better deal. And soon the newcomers began trading with the Native Americans for something even more valuable than fur. Can you guess what it was?

By the 1800s, settlers were coming from Europe by the thousands to what had now become the United States of America. These settlers weren't really interested in furs or even gold—they wanted land! They looked at their new nation as a place of wide-open spaces that was theirs to take if they wanted, sometimes by trading goods with the Native Americans and other times by just taking without asking first!

The life of Native Americans had greatly changed. Once almost self-sufficient, or needing to trade only with each other, they had become dependent on trade with the colonists. Though Native Americans and colonists were at one time **interdependent** (that means they depended on each other for goods and services), the colonists came

to realize that they no longer needed the items that Native Americans had to trade—they could get these things from other colonies. That's how colonies became dependent on each other, just as regions of the United States now have to depend on one another for goods and services.

As our tour of America returns to the present, we'll see how people in Minnesota watch news broadcasts that are aired in New York and people in Wyoming drink orange juice made in Florida. In other words, we all need each other.

In the early 1800s, plentiful land attracted many settlers to the United States, where they established farms and grew many different crops.

3 The Northeast: Blueberries, Books, and Banks

Our tour of the present day United States begins in the Northeast, where the smallest state, Rhode Island, and the largest city, New York City, are located. In this region, small farms, some still with the stone fences built by the early colonists who once lived there, are only a short drive from huge cities, where millions of people now live.

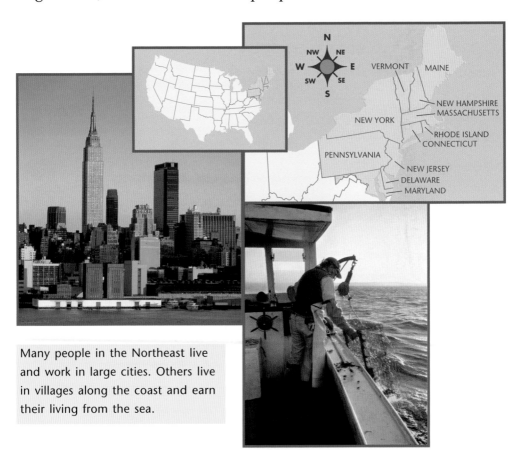

Many people in the Northeast live and work in large cities. Others live in villages along the coast and earn their living from the sea.

The economy of the Northeast depends upon a variety of natural and manufactured products.

Apples, blueberries, and cranberries are grown in this region. Factories in the Northeast produce glass, plastic, submarines, and helicopters. Many of the books and newspapers that you read are published in the Northeast, and the delicious maple syrup that people put on their pancakes comes from northeastern forests. Lobster, crab, and other seafood are caught by fishing boats off the shores of tiny villages that are found up and down the Atlantic coast.

New York City, home to nearly 10 million people, is the center of the **communications** industry and banking in the United States.

The plentiful variety of natural resources in the Northeast helps the United States economy in a big and special way, but as you'll soon learn, the other regions are also important. So let's continue the tour.

4 The Southeast: Orange Juice, T-shirts, and Good Times

The sweet scent of orange and peach blossoms fills the air as we pass through groves and orchards. Oranges and peaches will be shipped from Florida and Georgia to supermarkets throughout the United States. Factories will process some of the fruit to make juice and other fruit products.

In addition to oranges and peaches, crops such as peanuts, sweet potatoes, rice, and sugarcane are grown in the Southeast. This region's factories busily produce furniture, carpeting, paper products, and clothing. In fact, the T-shirt you might have put on this morning could have been made in the Southeast. Cities like Nashville and Atlanta provide things that most of us enjoy—country music and soft drinks. Shrimp boats leave their docks at least twice a day and spread their nets in the sea from the Carolinas to Louisiana, making fishing an important industry in the Southeast.

But what about the wonderful climate? When the chilly winds and freezing snows of winter arrive, some families from the cold climates of the Northeast and the Midwest head south. Warm sunshine, exciting theme parks, and natural beauty attract thousands of visitors to the Southeast every year. The business of providing vacations for others is a multi-million dollar industry called **tourism**, and it, too, has an important role in the economy of the United States.

Next stop—a "windy" city, lots of cows, and sunflower fields that brighten the prairie.

5 The Midwest: Farms and Factories

Welcome to the Midwest, often called "breadbasket for the world" and "America's heartland." (It's called this because this area is in the middle of the country, just like your heart is in the middle of your chest.) The land of the Midwest region is generally flat and covers most of the center of the United States. Its vast stretches of rich soil near the Great Lakes and the Mississippi River produce most of the food eaten in the United States.

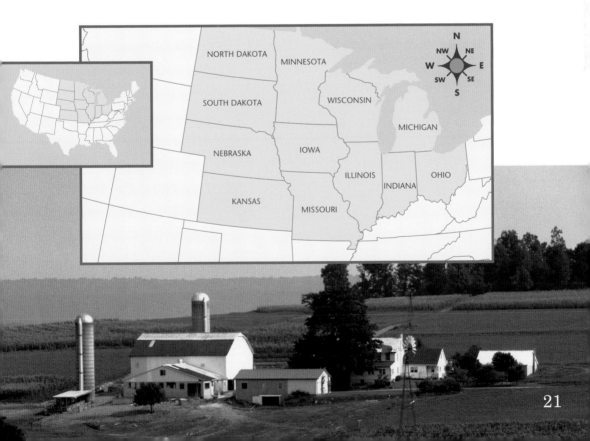

Wheat, rye, barley, and corn crops are plentiful on Midwest farms. Besides grain crops, the Midwest's rich soil produces apples, soybeans, cherries, and asparagus. Dairy and hog farms also contribute to the Midwest's huge food production.

Midwest factories produce a variety of products—from farm machinery to hot air balloons to automobiles. Like the Northeast, the Midwest has its share of large cities, such as Cleveland, Detroit, Minneapolis, and Chicago, the third largest U.S. city. Chicago, often called the "Windy City," is a center for the publishing and transportation industries.

We just have two more regions to visit, so hang in there—you'll be glad you did!

Chicago, located on Lake Michigan, is called the "Windy City." There's often a breeze blowing off the lake.

6 The Southwest: Wide Open Spaces

The first thing most people notice when coming to the Southwest is that there is so much open land. In the Southwest, cattle graze on huge ranches, and vast fields of cotton and other crops soak up rays of blazing sunshine. But what really makes this region so rich isn't cattle or cotton—it's oil! Fields of oil wells fill much of the land in Texas and Oklahoma.

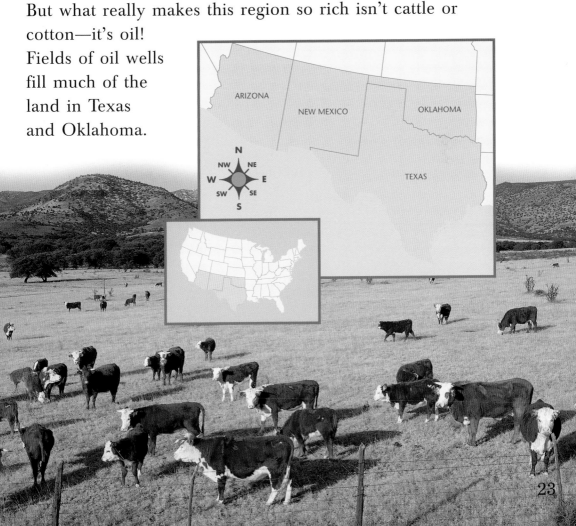

In addition to the cattle, cotton, and oil of Texas and Oklahoma, the southwestern states of Arizona and New Mexico have large copper, silver, and gold mines. Factories in this region produce a variety of goods, such as jewelry, aircraft, and missiles.

An important factor in the Southwest's economy is the Houston Ship Channel, a 50-mile-long waterway that links

Houston with the Gulf of Mexico. Huge oil, paper, and steel factories, as well as other industries, have grown in this area. Houston, the largest city in Texas and the busiest port in the United States, **imports** (brings to the United States) goods that are manufactured or grown in other countries and **exports** (ships from the United States) goods produced on farms and in factories across the country.

7 The West: Forests and Make-Believe

As we head west, we see big blue skies, mountains that climb over two miles high, and rivers that wind through some of the most beautiful land on Earth. Natural resources play an important role in the economy of the Northwest.

Thick forests that will someday produce a huge supply of lumber for building homes and schools flourish in the cool, damp climate of the West's coastal region. The business of growing trees and then making them into lumber is called forestry. Apple and cherry orchards grow well here, too, providing fruit for the nation.

In the early morning hours, fishing boats leave their docks up and down the Pacific coast, each crew hoping for a good catch. Fishing is one of Alaska's most important industries and produces seafood such as salmon, shrimp, crab, and cod.

A large net filled with salmon is hauled aboard this small fishing boat.

Though the wealth of natural resources found in the United States is extremely important in making our country strong, it's really the people who live in each region that are actually our country's most important resource. California's Silicon Valley is a good example of the talented people who work very hard to create better and faster computers and think of new ways to use them.

No visit to the West would be complete without a stop in Hollywood, California, where most of the movies you see are made. Here we can watch the actors and filmmakers who create the magic and make-believe in the movies and TV shows that thrill and entertain us. So let's sit back and enjoy the show!

Now that you've seen all of the United States, do you think our country has everything we need or want? Take a quick look around your room. Your bed was probably made in the Southeast from wood that came from a forest in the West. The books on your shelf were most likely created in the Northeast. What about the silver picture frame on your nightstand? Mines in the Southwest probably produced the silver to make it. Remember breakfast this morning? The wheat that was used to make the toast that you ate was likely to have been grown in the Midwest. Each region of the United States has made an important contribution to your daily life.

8 Who's Right?

Think back to the early Native Americans. At first most of these groups grew and gathered their own food and made their own clothing and tools. But then these groups began to move from place to place, and they met different Native American groups and later colonists and settlers who had different things that they thought would be useful to them. So what did these groups do? They traded, and that's how this country's economy began.

These Native Americans became interdependent in much the same way that the present regions of the United States depend on one another today. We depend on the farmers who grow food, as well as the factory workers who process and pack it. We need carpenters, plumbers, and electricians to build our homes, hospitals, and schools. We rely on doctors, nurses, and medicines to keep us healthy, mail carriers to deliver our mail, and the police and firefighters to protect us. In other words, we truly need each other.

The Five Regions of the United States				
	Features		Products	
	Climate	Natural Resources	Manufactured	Farm
Northeast	mild to hot summers, cold winters	forests	glass plastic submarines books	apples blueberries cranberries
Southeast	hot, humid summers, mild winters	rich soil	furniture appliances carpeting clothing	oranges peaches peanuts sweet potatoes
Midwest	mild to hot summers, cold winters	rich soil waterways	farm machinery cars hot-air balloons	wheat corn soybeans asparagus
Southwest	hot, dry summers, mild winters	oil grassland minerals	oil products steel missiles chemicals jewelry	cotton cattle
West	mild to hot summers, mild to cold winters	forests rich soil	computers aircraft	apples cherries lettuce grapefruit

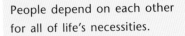

People depend on each other for all of life's necessities.

Because the United States has such a wealth of natural resources and can produce so many things that its citizens need, some people think that buying goods from other countries isn't necessary and will take business away from U.S. companies, resulting in a weaker economy, not stronger.

Other people believe that bringing goods in from other countries helps our economy because it provides competition and keeps prices down. And as communication and technology bring the nations of the world closer together, trading with other countries makes good sense.

The two biggest trading partners of the United States are Canada, to the north, and Mexico, to the south. We trade items such as manufactured goods, computer parts, and lumber goods with Canada. And we trade automobile parts, silver, and many other goods and services with Mexico.

Who's right? Should the United States trade with other nations? Read the two different points of view on the following pages, then decide for yourself.

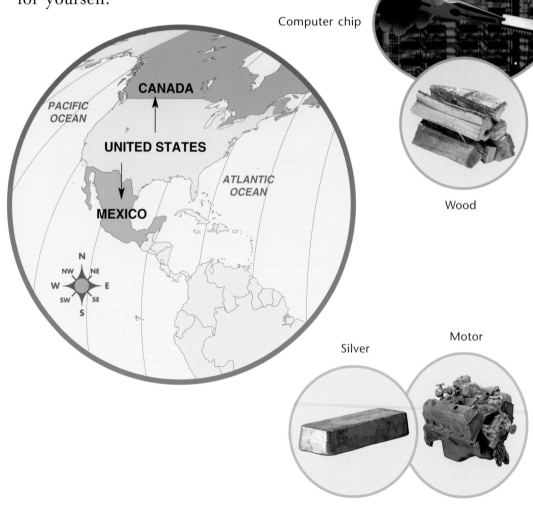

Computer chip

Wood

Silver

Motor

A Vote for Worldwide Trade

Many Americans say that trading with other countries is necessary for keeping the U.S. economy healthy. By trading, American businesses can obtain and sell goods not produced in the United States.

Some also argue that importing goods from outside of the United States provides competition and helps keep prices down. If we import similar goods from other countries that are less expensive than American goods, American companies will have to match these lower prices or buyers will choose the cheaper, imported items. After all, we all look for a bargain, don't we?

Free trade provides a variety of products at fair prices.

Besides bringing goods into the United States, trading with other countries provides a market for American products. Many industries in the United States produce more goods than we actually need. Trading with other countries strengthens these companies by providing another group of people who will buy their goods.

Finally because the United States has such a strong economy, many people believe that it also has a responsibility to support the economic growth of smaller, poorer countries. Computers link countries around the world, creating a worldwide economy that has made nations more interdependent than ever before. Creating a strong world economy will only help the United States.

Workers put together computers that help link countries around the world.

Safe working conditions and fair wages are important for workers in every country.

A Vote Against Worldwide Trade

Although items imported from other countries are often less expensive than those made in the United States, some people point out that they may be the result of unfair job conditions. Some developing countries do not have the same laws that we have to protect workers in America. In some places, people work for long hours under poor conditions, earning wages that are too low to support their families. Many Americans feel that the working conditions for these people will never improve as long as the United States continues to buy cheap goods produced this way.

Some Americans feel that buying goods from other countries rather than buying products made at home will harm U.S. businesses. Many fear that if we are able to get goods at low prices from foreign countries, there will be less need for goods that are made in the United States, and many of our factories might close. There would be fewer jobs for our workers, and the money they would have earned would go instead to people in other countries.

Workers sometimes gather to demand fair treatment. They work together to keep companies from closing.

Others argue that companies in some foreign countries are not concerned that they pollute the air and water supplies during the manufacturing process. Some American companies feel that since they have to pay for modern pollution controls, this brings the cost of their goods up. Because many factories in other countries are not required to pay for these controls, they can produce goods more cheaply and sell them at a lower price.

Now you decide. Who's right? Should we trade with other nations or should we keep all our wonderful resources to ourselves?

Factories must install special equipment to help control pollution.

Glossary

barter to trade things of equal value

colonist an early settler who came to America from another country

communication system of sharing information by radio, television, and so on

economy a country's system of producing, delivering, and using goods

export to ship goods out of a country for use in another place

import to bring goods into a country from another place

interdependent individuals or groups relying on each other for support

produce to make or provide something

tourism the business of providing services for travelers

trade to exchange goods or services

Index